SUGGESTIONS

for the Applicant

A Guide through the Job-Seeking Process

Michael Griffith

A simple overview of job hunting strategy for the job seeker.

ISBN: 978-1-105-11021-4

www.lulu.com/spotlight/mgriffith081

www.linkedin.com/in/michaelgriffithjr

Preface

My experience in Human Resources has always, in some way, had a recruitment element to it. Having staffed multiple projects and positions, and developed teams within organizations from the ground up, I have performed numerous searches for various positions. The chapters that I will address in this book are based on my own experiences and will hopefully provide ideas and insight to anyone seeking employment.

This is not intended to be an in-depth study of every issue you will encounter while searching for a job and going through the interview process. I do not believe that the average job seeker is concerned with this. I believe the average job seeker wants to know what to do, how to do it, what not to do, and how to avoid it.

This book is intended to be simple and to the point. There are examples for every suggestion in this book.

This book is titled "Suggestions" for these reasons. These are simple suggestions for anyone seeking a job. My hope in writing this book is to enable you to be strategic and effective in obtaining meaningful employment.

Table of Contents

Chapter 1: Resume

In my short time in Human Resources, the majority of my experience has been involved in some way with recruitment. I do not think that a Human Resources professional in a healthy organization will ever stop recruitment involvement. I have seen thousands of resumes and a resume is the key to attracting a potential employer to a candidate.

The purpose of this chapter is to offer my perspective on creating an effective resume. I have seen resumes ranging from hand written in pencil on scrap paper to laminated professional portfolios with real-life work samples. This is purely subjective, but below are the points I would recommend to anyone seeking a job to aid in the creation of an effective resume.

Design
The design is the least important feature of a resume. Any word processor will have multiple templates from which to choose, and the truth is that the design or layout is the least important part of resume creation. The content is the most important element of your resume. Focus your efforts on accurately portraying professionally who you are, what you have done, and what you want to do.

One element of design that requires thought is your font choice. Times New Roman, Arial, or something comparable is best. It is standard in business and easy to read on a screen or on paper. No Comic Sans.

Contact Information
Email Address
Your email address will say a lot about you. If you are applying for any type of professional, administrative, or management position, then choose an email address that appears profession. For sure, choose an email address that does not appear unprofessional. I have seen email addresses with things like "squirrel, big daddy, gurlz, dude", and anything else that

would make a resume screener think twice about taking a candidate's interest seriously.

Give a professional email address, even if you have to create a new one. There are numerous sites that give free email addresses. Use them. First.Last @ whatever.com. Last.First, Initial.Last, etc. Any combination of your name will be perfect.

Do not use numbers. Even if it is the year of your birth, don't do it. I don't want to know your age, your marital status, your hobby or interest, or anything else, especially from your email address. I want to know where I can send an email so that it will reach you. No one's home address is Bigdawg53 Dallas, TX.

Please do not use your work email address. Respect your current employer's email policies by choosing a personal address. Of the many reasons to not use a company work address, the first two that come to mind are:

1. You do not want your IT department to catch communication from you and a prospective employer. This could jeopardize your current position.
2. If I hire you, will you drag my company's domain through the mud by doing the same once you are employed at my company?

Phone

One phone number will suffice. Give the number where you can most conveniently be reached the majority of the time. For the same reasons as with the email address, use a personal number, not a work cell.

Other

If you have a solid LinkedIn profile, I would list the address to it. This can be found by logging into LinkedIn, going to "View Profile", and copying the "Public Profile" address. If you have a personal website that showcases your professional experience, list the web address.

Objective/Summary/Overview

I do not like objective statements. I know your objective. It is to get a job. Instead, I prefer summary or overview statements. This is who I am, this is what I have done, and these are, in short, my qualifications. Summary statements should be 4-5 sentences and 1 paragraph.

If you have recently graduated from university, state that. Something like *Recent graduate of School Name seeking first professional opportunity to gain exposure to real world scenarios that bring to life my textbook studies from the past 4 years*. List core coursework and classes, any special projects, internships you have had, any certifications, etc. If you are entry level, mid career, or a seasoned professional, tell me how many years of experience you have in the field for which you are applying.

Professional Experience

Title of Section

Name this section "Professional Experience". This is kind of semantics, but I think it's the most professional (pun) title. Not work history, not past experience, etc.

Company Name

List the company that is on your paycheck. If you work for a subsidiary of a large company, state the company for whom you work(ed), then say *A subsidiary of....* If you are the design manager for a $100mm project for a subsidiary of a $5bb company, implying that you are the design manager for the parent company may hurt your chances in that a potential employer may think that you are extremely over qualified and most likely too expensive.

Dates of Employment

List the beginning month, ending month, and year of employment with each company. If this is your current position, the end date should be "Present". Unless you were with the company for more than 5 years, do not just list the years.

Title(s)

If you have had more than one position or title with a company, list them all chronologically descending. Bold the most recent and list it first. For example, if you are an HR person and you began with Company ABC as a recruiter, moved into benefit administration, and then became a generalist, that is great information to know. It shows specialized and general experience as well as a career progression. List them all.

Consistency

Be consistent in your presentation of work experience. This will likely be the bulk of the content of your resume and without doubt will be the section that a potential employer spends the most time. Below are some points on consistency with work experience presentation:

- Bullets - If you use bullets to point out specific achievements, use bullets throughout the work history section. If you have worked for three companies, use bullets for all three. If you use bullets, use more than one per company.
- Paragraph - If you choose to write a paragraph about your experience with each respective previous employer, be precise and to the point.
- Period - Either end all bullets with a period, or end no bullets with a period. This shows attention to detail.
- Tense - Commit to a tense. All experience should be past or present tense. I recommend past for previous positions, since it was in the past, and for the current position, if you are still in that role, using present tense.

Action Words

Bullets in Professional Experience should start with action verbs of what you actually did. Examples of words to begin bullets with are "managed, directed, developed, designed, created, engaged, demonstrated, implemented, administered, oversaw, reviewed, compared..."

Accuracy

Do not lie in your resume. If your boss did it, don't say you did it. If you were part of a team that did it, say you were part of a team that did it. Besides the ethics of lying, you are setting yourself up for failure if you are selected for the position by claiming ability and experience that you do not have. This is unfair to the employer, obviously, but unfair to you and your career as well.

Internships

If you have graduated from college in the past 1 to 2 years, I think relevant internships add value to your experience and I would certainly have this on my resume.

Professional Competencies

This section can be titled different things. I would title it "Professional Competencies" or "Knowledge, Skills, and Abilities". I think that either of these most accurately reflects what the content will be, what the employer wants to know, and it is in line with most Job Description language.

Certifications/Licenses

If you hold any certifications, licenses, awards, continued education, or anything else relevant to your professional field, list it here. If you are an engineer with a Professional Engineer license, list it here. If you are in the IT or software development field and hold Microsoft, Java, or Cisco certification(s), list it here. If you are an HR professional and have a PHR or SPHR certification, list it here. If OSHA certifications are relevant to your industry and you have them, list them. If you are pursuing any certifications, list that you are pursuing them here. Professional memberships are another good thing to list in this section.

Relevance

Be relevant. If you are a software developer, tell me what programming languages you have used and how proficient you are in the language. If you are a construction project manager, tell me what your major accomplishments are by projects and project type (civil, industrial, commercial). If you are an IT professional, tell me about IT accomplishments.

If you are experienced and are applying for a position in the administrative/clerical field, I don't want to know about your real estate license. It is irrelevant and I don't care. If anything, I would think that you are hopping around in different industries.

Education

List the college which you attended, the date which you graduated (month and year), and the degree which you received. If you are still in the program, list the month and year of "Anticipated Graduation". If you did not graduate, but have over half of the credit hours and they were core classes for the degree you were pursuing, list the degree you were pursing, the number of hours achieved, GPA at departure, and relevant classes and coursework. If you took 1 to 2 semesters of a 4 year program 10 years ago, I don't want to know about it. I would think that you had 13th grade English, Math, History, and Science, and I can't think of any position that would benefit from another year of any of these.

GPA

◆   If your GPA was 3.0 or greater, list it.

◆   If your GPA was 2.0 to 3.0, I might not list it. Not to hide it, but it's not really a bragging point or highlight.

◆   If your GPA was less than 2.0, I would certainly not list it.

Other Information

Work Eligibility: If you require sponsorship, even if it is OPT (Optical Practical Training), say so. The employer will know this at some point anyway and it gets it up front at the beginning that the employer will have some additional administrative process if you are selected.

References: I do not think that references belong on a resume. I think references should be provided as a separate document. Whenever references are provided, they should be professional references. The best references are people whom you have directly reported to. Additional references can be someone who has reported to you and colleagues with whom you have worked. Do not list family members, friends, college professors (unless you have recently graduated), or college classmates.

Salary History: I do not think that salary history belongs on a resume. I think that salary history should be provided at a later stage in the pre-employment process. A salary history should show base wages, bonus earned (not potential), 401K or other retirement matching, and any other form of compensation such as benefit premiums paid by the company, company vehicle, auto allowance, fuel/gas card, cell phone, etc.

What NOT to Include on a Resume

Again, this is all subjective and my personal preference, but below are things that I have seen on resumes that contribute nothing to a candidate's hire-ability:

◆   Golf handicap. I have no idea why, but someone listed their golf handicap. This tells me that they play a lot of golf. Nothing more.

- Social clubs, fraternities, sororities, etc. Unless you are a recent graduate or you know for sure that the person making the hiring decision was a part of the same club, I do not know what value this shows other than a lot of extracurricular activity.

- Hobbies. I do not think listing hobbies is a terrible thing, but I don't know what value it provides to the position which you are applying. There are exceptions, but for the vast majority of instances, I think this is space filler.

- Age, Date of Birth, Nationality, Marital Status, Children, or anything else than could show a protected class. The truth is most employers want to evaluate candidates on their experience and abilities. They do not want to make a hiring decision based on anything else. So listing any of these details is irrelevant to the job.

- Reason for leaving previous employer. I would not put this on a resume unless you have worked 5 places in the past 2 years and have valid reasons for leaving so many positions. Valid reasons are things like contract positions, lay-offs, or anything else other than a standard voluntary or involuntary termination.

- Irrelevant work experience. Unless you have just graduated from college, I don't want to know about part time bar-tending, pizza delivery, lawn maintenance, retail sales, or fast food customer service experience. It's irrelevant. The reason I might put these on my resume if I just graduated college is to show that I did something while attending school.

Format

- Word Processor: I recommend creating your resume with a word processor. It should be saved in a .doc format. While most companies have adopted compatibility with .docx (Word 2007 and higher), not all have.

- PDF: If you have a resume layout that uses lines, borders, or an uncommon font, saving your resume as a pdf will preserve formatting.

- Web: I recommend having a web-ready version of your resume. A lot of employers, especially major employers, require applicants to apply on their website. Something as simple as the content of your resume broken down without formatting into a word or text document will be perfect. Have it ready to copy and paste into the boxes of employers recruitment sections of their website.

Things to Remember

♦ HR is your first filter. Not all HR professionals fully understand the industry in which they work and the desired profile for the position which they are filling. Carrying on for two pages with technical jargon will likely confuse the average HR resume screener. This is why precision is important.

♦ The intent of your resume is to get an interview. That's it. It is not your biography, it is not your philosophy on life or work, nor is it everything you have ever done professionally. It is a 1-to 2-page document that can lead to an interview.

♦ In as few words as possible, give me the most accurate representation of who you are, professionally, what you have done, and what you want to and can do for my company.

Closing

In summary, your resume is an introduction of yourself. You want an employer to see a knowledgeable professional who is competent in the field and industry in which you are applying and in which the company makes money. Every letter and every word on your resume should be carefully written with this in mind.

Appendix

♦ Sample Resume - Administrative Assistant
♦ Sample Resume - Accountant
♦ Sample Resume - Civil Engineer
♦ Sample Resume - IT Technician
♦ Sample Resume - Office Manager
♦ Sample Resume - Project Manager
♦ Sample Resume - Superintendent

Chapter 2: Networking

Now that you have created an effective resume, you have to get it out and noticed in the marketplace. The purpose of this chapter is to discuss networking strategies to find employment openings. I have filled hundreds and hundreds of positions over the past 6 years. I advertise my openings a very small percentage of the time. I rely on those who I have already hired to refer quality candidates who they have worked with in the past. This is networking from the employer's perspective.

From the applicant's perspective, this should work in reverse. Everyone you know personally, professionally, and socially is a network. Each of them has personal, professional, and social connections. You should tap into this network to find out about openings that have not been advertised. Additionally, you should try to connect with people with hiring authority in their company who may have a need that has not yet been opened as a requisition.

Employer Websites

Employer websites are the first places to start. If you are in a specialized, non-general field of vocation or industry, search for the top, local employers who would have positions for your profile. Create an account on the respective employer recruiting sites. It is time-consuming, but a great way to find open positions. Another advantage is that your profile will already be in the company's system when a position does become available.

Social Media

Social media is another great way to network. Invest some time in your LinkedIn profile. I would recommend that your social media profiles mirror your resume. Many social networking sites have "Jobs" sections. Some positions may be applied for with your profile information.

Once you have a solid profile, search for people on the site in your industry. Try to connect with them. Send messages asking about opportunities. Have pre-written introduction messages drafted so you can be consistent and precise with your message.

Find HR professionals in your area and with companies that you would like to work for. Again, try to connect and send messages to them. I get a lot of messages from my connections and from non-connections who are basically using the site as a way to express interest in my company. The shorter and precise messages make the most impact and have a better chance of being read and noticed.

Former Colleagues

Former colleagues are a great source of networking. People you worked with 5-10 years ago may have moved on to other companies and could be a great way to learn about opportunities and to be introduced to managers. If you left a previous company on good terms, it could be beneficial to contact a previous manager. Even if the former managers are still with your former company, they may have a network of other managers in the same industry outside of that company and could make an introduction for you.

Professional Associations and Societies

Just about every professional field has a professional organization. HR has SHRM. Engineers have societies of professional engineers and associations of discipline specific engineers. They usually have monthly lunches and other continued education events and seminars. Find out when and where they meet and try to go to the event. Have resumes and business cards in hand. Try to collect as many business cards as you can and follow up within a day or two. The goal is to keep communication moving and become connected or networked with more and more people.

Many associations and societies have websites for communication, articles, and other information relevant to the respective industry. This is also a great place to connect with peers. Many of these sites have jobs sections. If you work in a field where licensure or certification is important, the jobs section of a professional association or society would be a great place to find open positions.

Tracking

If you plan to network with these methods for the purpose of finding a job, you will hopefully meet a lot of new people and apply with numerous companies. Keep track of your progress. This will be good encouragement for your efforts and will also enable you to follow up with loose ends. A "Network Tracking Sheet" is included as an example in the appendixes section.

Getting an Interview

It is important to remember that the intent of all of this is to get an interview. Once you have connected with as many people as you can, you should be strategic and bold to get an interview. If you have applied on company websites for a position for which you are a fit, follow up with someone through your network who is at the company and could be part of the hiring authority. Ask specifically for an interview.

Another strategy is to go to the office of the company a few days after you have applied. If you know who posted the job through a social site or other network, ask the receptionist for them. If they are unavailable, continue to go back to the office. Once you do get a chance to speak with someone, be brief and to the point. Be direct: *My name is Michael Griffith and I applied for your HR position on your website and through LinkedIn. I wanted to stop by and drop off my resume. I am very interested in the position and the company. If you have a few minutes now or in the next week or two I would love the opportunity to speak about my experience.*

You may be concerned that you will be pestering or annoying someone. The truth is you are. However, once the annoyance has passed, any hiring manager or HR person will admire your boldness. By doing this you have shown initiative, creativity, and a desire for the position.

Appendixes
♦   Network Tracking Sheet

Chapter 3: Interviewing

Having staffed multiple projects and positions, and developed teams within organizations from the ground up, I have performed numerous interviews for various positions. The bullets that I will address are based on my own experiences and will hopefully provide ideas and insight to anyone who will be interviewed. My intent is to explain logic and strategy from the perspective of an employer conducting an interview.

Preparation

Preparation is a key element to succeed in an interview. There are several things you can do before an interview to prepare for the interview. Below are several things that I would recommend a candidate do before an interview.

Company

Wherever you interview, the most basic thing you can do is go to the company's website to learn about the company. Things that will help you determine your value to the company are:

♦ History: Learn as much as you can about the history of the company. When was the company founded? Who owns the company? Is it publicly traded? What are major projects that the company has completed?

♦ Identity: What are the company's vision, mission, and core values? Once you know these, do you believe in them? Can you support them?

♦ Product: How does the company make money? Unless you will be in the equivalent of the production department, you need to know how you can help the company make money and how you can support those who do.

Position

♦ Responsibilities: What are the key responsibilities of the position for which you are being considered? Ask Human Resources for a job description. Be prepared to answer questions and give examples of experience and ability for every bullet on the job description.

♦ Requirements: What are the main requirements of the position? Be prepared to show that you meet the requirements. The requirements may include years of experience, education, training, license, or certifications. They may include aptitude in software or knowledge of industry standards.

Interview Details

♦ Location: Look up the address and make sure that your route is correct. I have had many candidates late to an interview because their GPS routed them to the wrong place. Make sure you know where you are going.

♦ Time: Be on time. That sounds simple, but a lot of candidates mess it up. Don't show up an hour early and don't show up 15 minutes late. Get to the office 15 to 30 minutes ahead of time. Stay in your car and prepare yourself to interview. Walk into the office 5 minutes before your interview.

♦ Interviewers: Ask who the interviewers will be. Will you be meeting with Human Resources, a manager, multiple managers, etc?

♦ Dress Code: Ask for the appropriate attire. Men, it's awkward wearing a 3-piece suit when everyone else is in jeans. It's more awkward wearing khakis and a polo shirt when the people interviewing you are wearing ties. Ladies, cover your body as professionally as possible. If you're dressed for the club, it will not be in your favor.

♦ What to Bring: Bring something to write with, something to write on, and a copy or two of your resume.

Employer's Perspective

It is beneficial for the candidate to know what an employer is looking for in an interview. If you understand what the employer wants to know, then you can best prepare to tell them. An employer is looking for the following:

♦ Relevant Experience: An employer wants to fill their position with a candidate who has experience equivalent to the position being filled.

If the employer has an opening for a software developer who has worked on Department of Defense projects developing software, then the employer wants to know if you have experience developing software on DoD projects.

- Qualifications: With most positions, there are some basic qualifications relative to the position, that candidates must satisfy. This can be years of experience, education, training, license, certification, or aptitude with particular software or standards. The employer may require a Bachelor's degree in Journalism and 10 years of experience in the field. OSHA certifications or a professional engineer license from a state board of engineers may be required. High level ability in Excel, PrimaVera, Photoshop, Java, C#, or any other software may be required. Other requirements may be experience in and knowledge of industry standards for things like quality assurance, traffic control, etc.
- Trust: Other than the right set of Knowledge, Skills, and Abilities, an employer wants to feel like they can trust you. They want to feel some confidence that you will come to work, come to work on time, and do your job to the best of your ability.

With these things in mind, prepare for your interview by addressing these areas of your own experience. If you are deficient in one area, how can you compensate for it in another area?

Basic Interview Questions

Be prepared to answer the basic, common interview questions. By "be prepared", I mean have your answers memorized. There is no reason to not have answers prepared for the following questions:

- What experience do you have that is similar to the responsibilities of this position?
- What do you know about this company/project?
- Are there areas of this position where you are not as strong as you could be?
- Are there areas of this position where you have strengths?
- What sets you apart from the other candidates that I will interview?
- Why did you leave your last job?
- What did you like about your last boss?
- What did you dislike about your last boss?

- How well do you work under pressure and stress?
- What do you want your job title to be in 2 years/5 years/10 years?

These are not questions that I can suggest answers to. I think they will be different for everyone. My opinion is that honesty is the best policy. Just tell the truth. If you are good at something, I want to know that. If you are weak in some areas, tell me.

After the Interview

After the interview, be sure to follow up with those who interviewed you. Ask for business cards during the interview to obtain email addresses. Email the people who interviewed you within 24 hours of the interview. Thank them for their time and insight and reiterate your interest in the position. Summarize your qualifications for the requirements of the position. I would not recommend calling anyone who has not yet called you. Likely, you will have exchanged phone calls with Human Resources before the interview. It is appropriate to call Human Resources for status updates and follow up. I would probably not call a hiring manager unless they first called me.

Interview Dos

Below is a list of things you should definitely do during an interview:

- If you want the position, say so. Once a clear understanding of the position has been given and the interview is nearing the end, if you want the job, state so plainly. *I want this job. If there is any doubt about my ability to perform this job, please tell me now so that I may address your concerns.*
- Ask questions about the position. Ask what a typical day or week would entail. Ask about challenges that the position will face.
- Ask the interviewers what they are looking for in a candidate.
- Ask what the expectations of this position would be the first month, 3 months, 6 months, and year. Write down the answers. If you get the job, make sure you deliver.
- Be frank about your strengths and be frank about your weaknesses.

Interview Don'ts

Below is a list of things you should NOT do during an interview:

- Lie. Do not lie about your experience. Stretching the truth, exaggerating, embellishing, etc., are all synonyms for "lie". Do not lie.

If you get a job based on lies, you will likely end up where you are now, but with an involuntary termination on your record and wasted time that you cannot account for.

- Joke. Do not joke in an interview. I assure you that no hiring manager is looking for the candidate with the best sense of humor. You may be hilarious. The hiring manager may be hilarious. You can be hilarious together after you get the job.

- Avoid eye contact. If someone cannot look me in the eyes and tell me why I should hire them, I feel uneasy about their character.

- Give one-word answers. Elaborate. You should speak considerably more than the hiring manager in an interview. It is true that you are also interviewing the company. But it is much easier for the company to sell you on getting a paycheck from them than it will be for you to convince them to pay you. You should speak with intent and thoroughly explain yourself at every opportunity.

Appendix

- Sample Interview Questions for the Applicant

Chapter 4: Career Fair Strategy

I have attended numerous career fairs over the past years and I always have the same goal. My goal is to speak with as many applicants as possible and learn as much about their past experience and future professional aspirations in as little time as possible.

My intent is to give strategies to make you stand out from the crowd. I want you to have the tools to make a lasting impression from a short conversation. We will discuss preparation, materials, and approach. Additionally, we will develop a strategy to meet the employer's perspective, to track progress, and to follow up after the fair.

Preparation

First, and most importantly, you need to be able to give a verbal overview of yourself as a professional in 60 to 90 seconds. This is your introduction. This is something that you should rehearse and memorize. It should flow freely and not feel forced. Your objective is to tell your education, employment history, professional and applicable abilities and skills, and your goals for the short and long future.

Introduction

Your introduction statement should say who you are, what you do, how long you have been doing it, and what you want. This is kind of like the first paragraph of a paper. Your introduction says, "This is what I am about to tell you more about." Examples of effective introduction statements are:

My name is Michael Griffith. I have a Bachelor's degree from Abilene Christian University. I have been in the Human Resources field for about 6 years, staffing administering human resources for construction and software development companies. I am pursuing my PHR certification and would like to be considered for a Generalist or Manager position with your company to work under and learn from a more senior Human Resources professional.

My name is Sally Smith. I have a Finance degree from the University of Texas. I received my CPA certification 4 years ago. I have worked in the Finance department of large companies for the past 10 years. I am about half way through my graduate degree and hope to be considered for the Controller position with your company.

My name is Peter Jones. I've worked on major road and bridge construction projects for the past 25 years. I have worked my way from laborer to Superintendent and am looking for a position as a Superintendent with your company.

If you have recently graduated from college, you should follow the same guidelines. An example of an effective introduction statement for a recent or upcoming graduate is:

My name is Jennifer Johnson and I will graduate in May with a Bachelor's degree in Construction Science. I interned with TXDoT as an inspector an intern field technician on different projects over the past 3 summers. I have been involved in multiple school projects taking a construction process from estimating, to scheduling, to execution. I would like to join your company to begin my career in construction management.

Education

Relevance is the key with your education and how much time you allot to speaking to it. If you are in the IT field and your degree is in Art History, it would be better to just say I have a Bachelor's degree from *School Name*. If you are in the Accounting field and you have an undergraduate degree in Finance, you definitely want to note the degree.

Employment History

If you have applicable work and industry experience, you should speak to that in as few words as possible. The company you have worked for, the title you held, and the 3 to 4 key responsibilities you managed are the bullets you want to state. The more you say about your employment history, the less the interviewer is likely to remember. You want to make a lasting impression by being as relevant to the company and position as possible.

We will discuss the benefit of researching the companies at the career fair later, but as part of this research, you should have introductions prepared for each company. If you are an accountant who has worked in different industries, talk more about the industry experience you have for the company with whom you are speaking. If you do not have relevant industry experience, speak more about your skill set as it applies to the position and not the industry.

Abilities

What are the key responsibilities of the position? What are the main requirements for consideration of the position? You should have answers for both of these questions for every employer with whom you will speak. Additionally, you should be able to highlight your experience with the responsibilities and show that you meet the requirements of the position.

Goals

Whether I am a representative at a college career fair or a general gathering, I want to know your goals for the next 1 to 5 years. This is a question I always ask. Your answer will tell me a couple of things. The first is whether or not you have aspirations that have been thought out. The second is that I will be able to determine if the position that I have available will put or keep you on a career path to meet your future goals. Your goals can be a job title, job function, education, certification or license, or anything else that you would like to accomplish professionally in the short and long future.

Research

Before the career fair, find out what companies will be present. Find out what positions they will be looking to fill. Learn as much as you can about the companies and the positions that will be represented at the fair. Create a priority list of the employers. This way your time can be best utilized at the fair. Start with the employer with whom you would most like to speak. Work your way down your list.

Company Specific Cover Resumes and Cover Letters

Once you have researched the companies and positions that will be represented at the career fair, you should prepare company-specific resumes and cover letters. This shows pre-thought and initiative and can make you stand out to a potential employer. For your resume, this can be as simple as adding a sentence in your summary/overview section. For your cover letter, you can speak to the company's business line, history, values, or anything else that has made you want to be a part of that team.

An example of a company-specific cover letter can be found in the appendixes section.

Approach to Employer

Now that you are prepared, it is time to approach the employer. Approach may not seem like a big deal, but when you have 2 to 5 minutes to make an impression with me that will last after I have spoken to hundreds of people in a 5-hour stretch, your approach is crucial. I have had applicants wander up to my booth and stare at my banner without saying a word. I have had applicants stand 10 feet back and wait to be beckoned. Rarely does someone walk up, reach out their hand, and say hello. Even rarer is the applicant who walks up, shakes my hand, and tells me in a few sentences who they are, what they have done, what they want to do, and how they can fit into the company that I represent.

This is exactly what you should do. I should not have to ask you who you are, what you want to do, or what you have done. This is the case, however, a high percentage of the time. I have to draw out of someone their experience and professional desires. I was recruiting at a major university in Texas a couple of years ago and a student who was going to graduate in a couple of months had the following exchange with me:

MG = Me
AP = Applicant

AP stands slightly in front of and beside my booth, staring at my company banner.

MG: *How are you?*
AP: *I'm good. What do you guys do?*

Mind you, the banner has people in hard hats, heavy machinery, and bridges and highways being constructed.

MG: *We build bridges and roads. What do you do?*
AP: *Oh. I graduate in May.*

Remember, this is February.

MG: *Well, what do you want to do when you graduate?*
AP: *I don't know. My dad does construction.*
MG: *What's your major?*
AP: *Engineering.*
MG: *What discipline?*
AP: *Civil.*

Silence….

I noticed the kid's last name and hometown from his resume, which he was still holding on to. I asked if he knew someone who was the VP of Engineering at a company I had worked for in the past. It was his father. That is, his dad who does construction.

I know your dad. I worked with him. I recruited a lot of people for him. What would he say if he knew that you were a few months away from graduation and that you were wandering around the engineering fair telling employers that you did not know what you wanted to do with the rest of your life?

The same year, I attended a general, non-college career fair. In many ways, this type of fair is much more difficult for the applicant. The reason is that employers will speak with a large variety of professionals. Also, the applicant will speak with a large variety of Employers. Below is an example of an awkward exchange with an unprepared applicant from this fair.

The applicant, who was wearing jeans and had sunglasses on top of his head, stood directly in front of my booth staring at the handouts on the table in front of me.

MG: *How are you doing?*
AP: *I'm doing.*

MG: *Do you have a resume?*
AP: *No.*

MG: *What kind of position are you looking for?*
AP: *I don't know. I just thought I'd come over and see what you guys were all about.*

Keep in mind that the majority of the applicants at this fair were unemployed. As we discussed in the interview section, it is important to make sure that an employer is a good fit for you, but in no way are you interviewing a company at a job fair. The company is interviewing you.

Don't be either of these people. Come to me, tell me who you are, what you have done, what you want to do, and what qualifies you to do it. I should have to ask for very little when you only have 5 minutes to convince me to bring you back for an interview.

I will always ask you what you know about my company. You should have an answer for this for every company with whom you will speak. There is no good reason to not be prepared.

Employer's Perspective

So what is the employer looking for in a career fair? The Employer will speak with hundreds of Applicants in a condensed amount of time. From the Employer's perspective, Career Fairs are not fun. I have to shake a lot of hands, stand up all day, and have the same conversation over and over for 3 to 6 hours.

I am looking for someone who is prepared. The ideal Applicant at a Job Fair should know something about my Company and what we do to make money. They should take initiative to approach me and tell me what type of position they are looking for. They should be able to summarize their professional abilities, previous employment, and future goals in 60 to 90 seconds. If someone does this and hands me a decently written resume, as long as I have a position that they might fit, they will be called back for an interview.

Tracking

When you attend a career fair, you will likely speak with a lot of companies. Keep track of who you spoke to and what you spoke about. Keep track of the positions that were open. Collect business cards or contact information from every company you meet with. A "Career Fair Tracking Sheet" is included as an example in the Appendixes section.

After the Career Fair

Your work has only just begun once the career fair has ended. Use your network tracking sheet and the methods discussed in the Interviewing and Networking chapters to follow up with employers. The Career Fair Tracking Sheet will be a useful tool in tracking your progress and will aid you in building relationships with prospective employers.

Appendixes

♦ Company Specific Cover Letter
♦ Career Fair Tracking Sheet

Chapter 5: Supporting Documents

In addition to your resume, there are a number of other documents that may be requested from the prospective employer. In some cases, though they might not be requested, it is good to submit documents in addition to your resume to give the prospective employer as much information about your professional background as possible.

I recommend having all of the documents that we will discuss prepared and easily accessible in a number of different formats. You should have these prepared and stored electronically and in hard copy formats. The goal is to have everything ready so that you can quickly submit information as it is needed.

I recommend consistency in your resume and supporting documents. Use the same font type and size. Use the same header and footer if you have them. If you bold certain things in your resume, bold the same type of things in your supporting documents. If you use special characters for bulleting lists in your resume, use the same bullet types in your supporting documents.

Introduction/Cover Letter

The purpose of an introduction or cover letter is to open the door of communication with an employer. An introduction letter should include a lot of the same information as your resume, but with less detail, and it should flow as a narrative rather than a list.

Your introduction/cover letter should include your contact information. The same rules apply to your resume. Give your name, address (city and state), email address, and phone number.

If you know the name of the person whom you will submit your information, address this person directly in the greeting of your letter. If you do not, safe alternatives are:

To Whom It May Concern,

Sir or Madam,

Dear Hiring Manager,

Your first paragraph will be much like your 60-to 90-second career fair introduction. This should be a quick statement of who you are, what you have done, what you would like to do, and what qualifies you to do it.

Your second paragraph should tell the employer how you can benefit their company. Say something about the company that you like. This can be the company's mission, vision, or core values, projects, reputation, etc.

Spend a paragraph for each of your previous positions. Highlight achievements, responsibilities, and the reason you left the employer. Good reasons to have left a company are for opportunity to gain more experience, lay off or reduction in force, moving out of the area, or something similar. I would not say things that are degrading to your previous company or past co-workers and managers.

Your last paragraph should be a recap of your qualifications. You should state your interest with the company and in the position. Additionally, you should state your time frame of availability and desire to hear back from the employer.

Your salutation should be simple and professional. This letter should not end with the same salutation as if you were writing a friend, family member, or spouse. I point this out because I have received cover letters with *Truly yours*, *With peace and love*, and other things that do not represent a professional. Appropriate salutations are *Respectfully*, *Sincerely*, *Best regards*, or anything along those lines. A sample Introduction/Cover Letter is included in the Appendixes section.

References
Most professional positions with reputable companies will at some point in the recruitment process ask you for references. It is good to have these

prepared ahead of time and have formatting consistent with other documentation that you have submitted.

Appropriate references are usually someone you have worked with, someone you have worked for, and someone who has worked for you. Previous managers are great references. They will have the most insight to a potential employer as to your abilities, performance, and potential. Inappropriate references are pretty much anyone else. Your mother, brother, buddy, running partner, or even college professor if you have been out of college for over 3 years are not appropriate references. These references will likely have no insight to your professional experience and abilities.

Make sure that the references you give know that they are being used as references. This might remind them to answer calls from unknown numbers. It will give you a chance to confirm the contact information that you are submitting. It will also allow them time to think about what they will say. You do not want to list a reference who is not expecting to be contacted or whose contact information is incorrect. A sample References page is included in the Appendixes section.

Salary History (Compensation History)

I was several years into my career before a salary history was requested. The first company I worked for never requested a complete compensation history from candidates other than what was standard on an employment application. There are a lot of benefits for you and for the employer in requesting this. An effective compensation history will give an mployer the most comprehensive view of your past conditions. It will also enable you to better leverage your previous pay with the pay you are requesting.

A salary history should include your total compensation package for every past position. You should begin with your base annual salary. If your beginning and ending base annual salaries were different, list both of them. Other things to list are:

♦ Bonus or potential bonus amount or percentage
♦ 401K or other retirement contributions made by the company
♦ Medical or other insurance premiums paid by the company

- Paid time off (Number of Vacation, Sick/Personal, and Holidays per year)
- Employer provided vehicle
- Employer paid fuel
- Employer provided cell phone
- Profit sharing or ESOP ownership

A sample salary history is included in the Appendixes section.

Licenses, Degrees, Transcripts, and Certifications

For specialized positions, or if you are a recent graduate, your transcript may be requested. If you are in a position that requires a license, it will most likely be requested. Your degree may be requested as well for verification. If your position requires any type of certification related to your field, industry, or safety area, it will be requested as well. It is good to have copies of all applicable license, degrees, transcripts, and certifications readily available. It is also good practice to have copies stored electronically to save time finding a scanner when they are requested.

Appendixes

- Sample Introduction/Cover Letter
- Sample References
- Sample Salary History

About the Author

Michael Griffith has held titles of Recruiter, Recruitment Manager, Generalist, and Human Resources Manager. He has worked for small, medium, and large companies with Human Resources Departments ranging from fully established with multiple senior managers to companies with no Human Resources practices defined. He has developed recruitment plans, benefit programs, compliance initiatives, policy and procedure, forms and templates, training and development plans, compensation structures, and other basic Human Resources administration processes.

Appendixes

First Last | **City, TX | First.Last@mail.com | 888-555-1234**

Summary

Experienced administrative professional seeking position in administrative and clerical field. 6 years of experience with office management, reception, administrative and executive assisting.

Professional Experience

Executive Assistant | Company A
April 2009 to Present

- ❖ Reserve flights and travel accommodations for senior executives.
- ❖ Coordinate schedule and calendar for multiple managers.
- ❖ Prepare internal communications and newsletters.
- ❖ Take notes from board meetings.
- ❖ Manage company events schedule and communications.

Office Manager | Company B
June 2007 to April 2009

- ❖ Order supplies, furniture, and other office items.
- ❖ Schedule maintenance for company equipment.
- ❖ Receive and distribute mail.
- ❖ Pack, box, and send mail.

Administrative Assistant | Company C
August 2005 to June 2007

- ❖ Answer calls and route to appropriate personnel.
- ❖ Prepare emails and other written communications.
- ❖ Take notes from meetings.
- ❖ Screen mail and other correspondence.

Professional Competencies, Certifications, and Other Qualifications

- ❖ Notary Public
- ❖ 10 Key
- ❖ Typing 85 WPM
- ❖ Microsoft Office Suite (Word, Outlook, Excel, Power Point)

Education

- ❖ Sample Junior College
  - ➤ Associates Degree, 2005

First Last **City, TX | First.Last@mail.com | 888-555-1234**

Summary

Experienced accountant in areas of A/P, A/R, payroll, and subcontract payable management. Familiar with industry standards and accounting principles. Knowledgeable in IRS rules and regulations.

Professional Experience

Accountant | Company A
June 2005 to Present

- ❖ Prepared quarterly indirect budget.
- ❖ Entered budget forecasts into accounting system.
- ❖ Prepared and processed pay requests.
- ❖ Tracked and filed W-9s, insurance, and subcontracts.

Accounting Administrator | Company B
December 2003 to June 2005

- ❖ Processed Accounts Payable and Accounts Receivable for subcontractors and prime contractors.
- ❖ Originate and maintain all subcontractor files.
- ❖ Processed change orders and pay requests.

Payroll Clerk | Company C
October 2002 to December 2003

- ❖ Processed payroll for 300+ employees on weekly and monthly basis.
- ❖ Entered invoices into accounting software.
- ❖ Reconciled invoices.

Professional Competencies, Certifications, and Other Qualifications

- ❖ E-OBRA
- ❖ Quickbooks
- ❖ Timberline
- ❖ Accrual Based Accounting
- ❖ MS Office

Education

- ❖ College State University
  - ➢ Some course work completed
  - ➢ Business Administration

First Last, P.E.   City, TX | First.Last@mail.com | 888-555-1234

Summary

Experienced civil engineer with 10 years of experience in the design of large heavy highway, bridge and highway projects. I have demonstrated advanced ability in the design of structures, roadways, drainage, traffic control, and geotechnical aspects of large projects. I am skilled in Microstation and AutoCAD, and have Professional Engineer licenses in Texas and Oklahoma.

Professional Experience

Structures Design Manager | Company A
January 2008 to Present
Responsible for the design of a major interchanges and retaining walls on Highway X in Dallas, TX.
- Prepared civil designs and field changes for multiple bridges and retaining walls.
- Designed signage and pavement markings for new construction.
- Produced submittals for client approval.

Traffic Control Design Engineer | Company B
April 2004 to January 2008
- Developed plans compliant with MUTCD specifications for traffic control.
- Designed temporary and permanent signage and pavement markings for multi-phase traffic control plans.
- Coordinated plan implementation to field management for traffic control.

Engineer in Training | Company C
January 2001 to April 2004
- Worked under the direction of a senior engineer to make design changes during construction.
- Developed drainage plans for State Highway project.
- Produced plans for review for preconstruction activities.

Professional Competencies, Certifications, and Other Qualifications
- Licensed Professional Engineer, TX (Number 123456789)
- Licensed Professional Engineer, OK (Number 123456789)
- Microstation, AutoCAD, GeoPak, Terramodel, Trimble

Education
- College State University
  - Bachelors Degree - Civil Engineering - December 2000
  - GPA   -   3.55

First Last   **City, TX | First.Last@mail.com | 888-555-1234**

Summary

Competent IT professional with 12 years of experience on the corporate side of IT management. Education, training, and experience in managing all aspects of corporate IT infrastructure. Experienced in the plan and execution of IT infrastructure development from the ground up.

Professional Experience

IT Manager | Company A
March 2005 to Present

- Implemented IT infrastructure for 3 subsidiary companies.
- Developed IT processes, policies, and procedures.
- Managed a team of 3 IT Technicians to provide network and desktop support to 300+ employees.
- Managed multiple remotely hosted and on site servers and environments.
- Managed a mobile user workforce of 300+ for Blackberry Enterprise Server.

Systems Administrator | Company B
June 2001 to March 2005

- Managed company IT infrastructure supporting local and remote users.
- Maintained 15 physical servers and over 250 virtual servers hosted on a VMWare ESX 3 environment.

IT Support Technician | Company C
February 1999 to June 2001

- Provided desktop support to users of Windows and Linux environments.
- Loaded computers with varying user applicable software and settings.
- Created virtual workstations.

Professional Competencies, Certifications, and Other Qualifications

Microsoft Windows Server NT/2000/2003/Windows NT/2000/XP	Microsoft SQL Server 2000-2008/Oracle DB
Microsoft Office	Cisco Routers/Switches
Microsoft Exchange Server 5.5/2003	Internet Information Server 3.0 +
Microsoft Remote Access Server	VMWare/VMWare ESX 3

Education

- College State University
  - Bachelors Degree - Information Technology – 1999

First Last | **City, TX | First.Last@mail.com | 888-555-1234**

Summary

Experienced Office Manager, administrative assistant, receptionist, and clerk in all areas of office administration and office support.

Professional Experience

Office Manager | Company A
December 2009 to Present

- ❖ Managed a team of 3 office support personnel.
- ❖ Developed office administration policies and procedures.
- ❖ Planned company events.
- ❖ Entered invoices into accounting system.

Administrative Assistant | Company B
November 2008 to December 2009

- ❖ Supported departmental manager.
- ❖ Coordinated manager's schedule.
- ❖ Drafted letters and other correspondence.

Receptionist | Company C
December 2006 to November 2008

- ❖ Greeted guests and visitors.
- ❖ Directed guests and visitors to meeting locations.
- ❖ Managed multi-line phone system and 100 extensions.
- ❖ Coordinated mail sending and receiving.

Professional Competencies, Certifications, and Other Qualifications

- ❖ Microsoft Word
- ❖ Microsoft Excel
- ❖ Microsoft Outlook
- ❖ 60 WPM
- ❖ Multi-line phone systems

First Last, P.E.   **City, TX | First.Last@mail.com | 888-555-1234**

Summary

Experienced civil engineer with 10 years of experience in the construction of large heavy highway, bridge and highway projects. I have demonstrated advanced ability in project estimates, baseline and critical path schedule development, bid review, subcontractor management, material and equipment procurement, quantity take-offs, design plan modification, traffic control development, change order administration, and claims management.

Professional Experience

Project Manager | Company A   January 2008 to Present

Responsible for the construction management of a major interchange on Highway X in Dallas, TX.

- ❖ Managed a $260mm project budget over 2 years
- ❖ Coordinated construction activities with the owner's representative
- ❖ Selected and managed subcontractors performing various works by discipline
- ❖ Directed a team of project engineers, superintendents, and other various departments

Project Engineer | Company B   April 2004 to January 2008

- ❖ Made changes to design plans to reduce time for construction
- ❖ Adjusted critical path schedule using PrimaVera
- ❖ Conducted field audits for quality control compliance

Field Engineer | Company C   January 2001 to April 2004

- ❖ Calculated estimates of quantity for material pricing and bid review
- ❖ Reviewed change orders for cost differences in field activities
- ❖ Assisted Project Engineer in schedule development
- ❖ Worked on a team of engineers for traffic control design

Professional Competencies, Certifications, and Other Qualifications

Licensed Professional Engineer (Number 123456789)	Competent Person Certified (2009)
Member of the TSPE	Certificate for MUTCD course
OSHA 500 Certified	Advanced ability in PrimaVera and Microsoft Project
OSHA Trench & Excavation Safety	Expert ability Word and Excel

Education

- ❖ College State University
  - ➢ Bachelors Degree - Engineering - December 2000
  - ➢ GPA - 3.25

First Last   **City, TX | First.Last@mail.com | 888-555-1234**

Summary

Seasoned Superintendent with 25 years of experienced in Civil and Commercial construction.

Professional Experience

General Superintendent | Company A

February 2000 to Present

Managed Small and medium size civil construction projects. Project highlights include:

- ❖ IH-635, Dallas, TX $41mm, paving and structures
- ❖ IH-45, Houston, TX $20mm, structures, new construction
- ❖ SH-130, Austin, TX $32mm, drilling and excavation
- ❖ DFW Airport runway, $15mm, paving and striping

Superintendent | Company B

May 1989 to February 2000

Directed foremen and field crews for multiple commercial construction projects in the Dallas, Houston, Austin, and San Antonio areas. Project types include:

- ❖ Multiple hotels
- ❖ Urban apartment complexes
- ❖ Municipal buildings
- ❖ Multi story office buildings

Foreman | Company C

October 1986 to May 1989

Directed various crews of unskilled and semi-skilled labor for city roads and small commercial projects.

Professional Competencies, Certifications, and Other Qualifications

- ❖ OSHA Certifications
- ❖ Computer literate
- ❖ Ability to interpret plans

Name	Position	Company	Email	Phone	Relationship	Date Contacted	Date Responded	Notes
John Smith	HR Manager	Company A	Jsmith@companyA.com	888-555-1234	LinkedIn	12/13/10	12/20/10	Possible position in early 2011
Jane Smith	Design Engineer	Company B	Jsmith@companyB.com	888-555-1235	Texas Society Professional Engineers	5/3/11	6/12/11	Forwarding resume to her mgr
Bob Smith	Sales Manager	Company C	Bsmith@companyC.com	888-555-1236	College	5/3/11	5/3/11	Nothing now but will keep in touch
Fred Smith	CFO	Company D	Fsmith@companyD.com	888-555-1237	Past Colleague	3/1/11	3/15/11	Mtg April 1
Kate Smith	IT Manager	Company E	Ksmith@companyE.com	888-555-1238	Past Boss	3/3/11		No response yet

Selection

1. What are the 3 or 4 key responsibilities and expectations for this position?
2. What are the most important requirements for a Candidate to posses to be selected for this position?
3. How soon would you like for someone to start?
4. Why is this position open?

Manager and Position

1. What will a typical day/week look like for this position?
2. What will be the biggest challenges for this position?
3. What has your experience and career progression been outside of, and within the company?
5. What would you expect from the person selected for this position the first month, 3 months, 6 months?

Company

1. What goals has the company established for the next year?
2. What projects, if applicable, is the company pursuing?
3. How has the company grown in employees and in revenue over the past 5 years?
4. What is the turnover rate for this position and for the company as a whole?

Compensation and Benefits

1. What is the base compensation range for this position?
2. Is this position eligible for potential bonus, and, if so, what is the percentage and how is the bonus determined?
3. What insurances and benefits does the company provide and how long is the waiting period for eligibility?
4. Will any training be provided by the company for this position in the short and long terms?

First Last   **City, TX | First.Last@mail.com | 888-555-1234**

Sir or Madam,

Thank you for your time reviewing my information. I have admired the values of your company and would love the opportunity to be considered for any position for which I may be a fit. I am particularly interested in your Dallas office. I have met several Accountants form this office at monthly CPA events and am impressed with the loyalty that they have to your company.

I have a Bachelor's degree in Finance from the University of North Texas. I have been in the accounting field for 10 years working for medium to large size companies. Most recently I have worked for one of your major competitors in the local market. I received my CPA certificate in 2008.

I have experience managing multiple accounting and finance procedures and responsibilities. Recently I have managed a department of 4 accountants directing activities and compiling reports for monthly board of manager meetings. I report directly to the CFO.

I am familiar with industry standards and knowledgeable in accounting principles. I have received corporate training and attend monthly seminars to stay up to date on laws, rules, and regulations.

I would like to work under the direction of a more senior finance and accounting professional to continue learning and developing in my field. I will begin pursuing my Master's degree in early 2012 with a projected completion date of 2015.

Thank you again for your time. I do hope to have the opportunity to meet with you to discuss my experience and how I might be a fit for your company. If there is any other information that I may provide, please let me know. I have attached my resume for your review.

Respectfully,

First Last

Name	Company	Fair	Available Position(s)	Email	Phone	Date Contacted	Date Responded	Notes
John Smith	Company A	Texas A&M	Construction Engineer, Project Controls, Design	Jsmith@companyA.com	888-555-1234	12/13/10	12/20/10	Possible position in early 2011
Jane Smith	Company B	University of Texas	Intern - Field and Office	Jsmith@companyB.com	888-555-1235	5/3/11	6/12/11	Forwarding resume to her mgr
Bob Smith	Company C	Dallas Area Fair	Office Admn	Bsmith@companyC.com	888-555-1236	5/3/11	5/3/11	Nothing now but will keep in touch
Fred Smith	Company D	Fort Worth Fair	Surveyor, CAD Technician, Drafter	Fsmith@companyD.com	888-555-1237	3/1/11	3/15/11	Mtg April 1
Kate Smith	Company E	Dallas Area Fair	Accountant, Book Keeper, CPA, Office Manager	Ksmith@companyE.com	888-555-1238	3/3/11		No response yet

First Last   **City, TX | First.Last@mail.com | 888-555-1234**

Sir or Madam,

Thank you for your time reviewing my information. My name is "First Last" and I have a Bachelor's degree in Finance from the University of North Texas. I have been in the accounting field for 10 years working for medium to large size companies. Most recently I have worked for one of your major competitors in the local market. I received my CPA certificate in 2008.

I have experience managing multiple accounting and finance procedures and responsibilities. Recently I have managed a department of 4 accountants directing activities and compiling reports for monthly board of manager meetings. I report directly to the CFO.

I am familiar with industry standards and knowledgeable in accounting principles. I have received corporate training and attend monthly seminars to stay up to date on laws, rules, and regulations.

I would like to work under the direction of a more senior finance and accounting professional to continue learning and developing in my field. I will begin pursuing my Master's degree in early 2012 with a projected completion date of 2015.

Thank you again for your time. I do hope to have the opportunity to meet with you to discuss my experience and how I might be a fit for your company. If there is any other information that I may provide, please let me know. I have attached my resume for your review.

Respectfully,

First Last

First Last   City, TX | First.Last@mail.com | 888-555-1234

Professional References

- ❖ Name: John Smith
- ❖ Relationship: Former Manager
- ❖ Company: Company A
- ❖ Title: Department Manager
- ❖ Email: JSmith@companyA.com
- ❖ Phone: 888-555-1234

- ❖ Name: Kate Smith
- ❖ Relationship: Former Manager
- ❖ Company: Company B
- ❖ Title: CFO
- ❖ Email: KSmith@companyB.com
- ❖ Phone: 888-555-1235

- ❖ Name: Jane Smith
- ❖ Relationship: Coworker
- ❖ Company: Company C
- ❖ Title: Software Engineer
- ❖ Email: JSmith@companyC.com
- ❖ Phone: 888-555-1236

First Last   **City, TX | First.Last@mail.com | 888-555-1234**

Compensation History

- ❖ Company: Company A
- ❖ Dates: April 2006 to Present
- ❖ Current Title: Sr. Project Manager
- ❖ Beginning Title: Project Manager
- ❖ Current Salary: $120,000.00 per Year
- ❖ Beginning Salary: $85,000.00 per Year
- ❖ Bonus Potential: 20%
- ❖ 401K Contribution: 3% of Salary
- ❖ Insurance Premium: $1,200.00 per Month
- ❖ Vehicle: Employer Provided Vehicle
- ❖ Paid Days Off: 30

- ❖ Company: Company B
- ❖ Dates: June 2001 to April 2006
- ❖ Ending Title: Sr. Project Engineer
- ❖ Beginning Title: Project Engineer
- ❖ Ending Salary: $80,000.00 per Year
- ❖ Beginning Salary: $62,000.00 per Year
- ❖ Bonus Potential: 10%
- ❖ 401K Contribution: 3% of Salary
- ❖ Insurance Premium: $900.00 per Month
- ❖ Vehicle: Auto Allowance
- ❖ Paid Days Off: 25

- ❖ Company: Company C
- ❖ Dates: December 1998 to June 2001
- ❖ Ending Title: Project Engineer
- ❖ Beginning Title: Project Engineer
- ❖ Ending Salary: $60,000.00 per Year
- ❖ Beginning Salary: $52,000.00 per Year
- ❖ Bonus Potential: 10%
- ❖ 401K Contribution: 3% of Salary
- ❖ Insurance Premium: $650.00 per Month
- ❖ Vehicle: N/A
- ❖ Paid Days Off: 25